P9-ECR-194

0 00

The Question & Answer Book

OUR WONDERFUL
SEASONS

OUR WONDERFUL SEASONS

By Elizabeth Marcus
Illustrated by Patti Boyd

Troll Associates

Library of Congress Cataloging in Publication Data

Marcus, Elizabeth.
    Our wonderful seasons.

    (The Question and answer book)
    Summary: Answers questions about the seasonal changes
produced by variations in the angle at which the sun's
rays strike the earth.
    1. Seasons—Juvenile literature. [1. Seasons.
2. Questions and answers] I. Boyd, Patti, ill. II. Ti-
tle. III. Series: Question and answer book (Troll
Associates)
QB631.M29 1983   525'.5   82-17372
ISBN 0-89375-896-5
ISBN 0-89375-897-3 (pbk.)

What is the story of the seasons?

The story of the seasons is a story of many wonderful changes. It is a story of the old and the new. It is a story of life.

Spring is a time of gentle rains and new beginnings. In the summer, the golden sunshine brings warmth and growth. Then come shorter, cooler days. It is autumn, and time for harvesting. In winter, everything seems to snuggle down to rest and wait. The sun seems far, far away, and the Earth waits for spring to come again.

What makes the seasons?

The seasons of the year come and go with a beautiful rhythm. But what makes the seasons? Part of the reason we have seasons is because of the way the sun shines on the Earth at different times of the year.

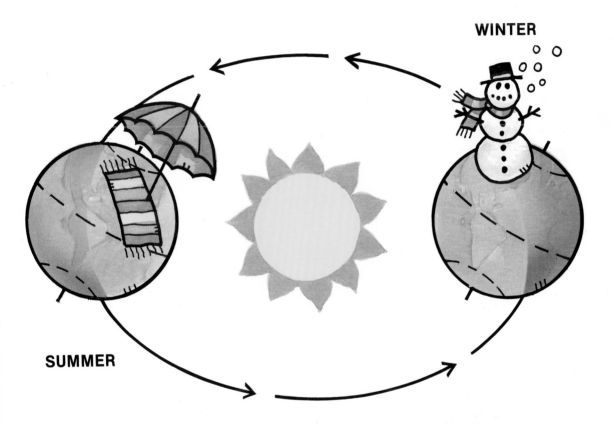

WINTER

SUMMER

In the summer in the northern part of the world, the sun's rays shine directly down on us. It looks very bright and feels very hot. In the winter in the northern part of the world, the sun's rays must travel at a slant to reach us. Slanted rays do not feel as hot or look as bright as direct rays. They seem to spread out more, so there is less heat and light.

You can see how a slanted beam of light spreads out if you try this simple experiment. All you need is a flashlight and a darkened room.

Stand about a foot (30 centimeters) away from a wall. Shine the flashlight straight at the wall. You will see a bright circle of light. The wall is receiving the direct light of the flashlight.

Now shine the same beam of light so it hits the wall at a slant. Look at the circle of light now. The light is spread out, so it covers much more space. When the wall is lit by the slanted beam of light, it is not as bright as when it was lit by the direct light.

The same thing happens with the sun's rays. Some places on the Earth receive the direct rays of the sun. Others receive slanted rays. The slanted rays of the sun are not as bright or as hot as the direct rays of the sun.

Why do different parts of the Earth receive different kinds of rays from the sun?

One reason is that the Earth is round, like a ball. The part of the Earth that bulges out toward the sun receives the most direct rays from the sun. The parts of the Earth that do not bulge out toward the sun receive slanted rays.

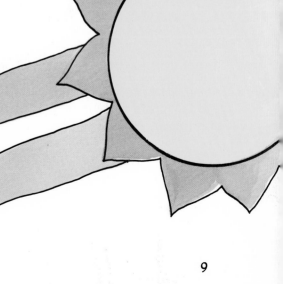

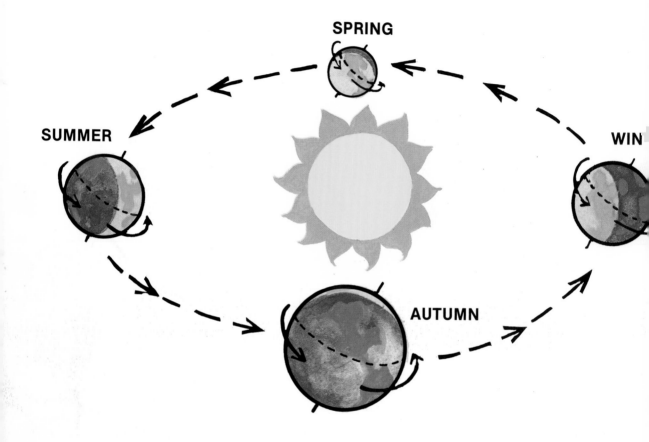

If the Earth stood still, the same part of the Earth would always bulge out toward the sun. But the Earth does *not* stand still. It moves—in two different ways. Different parts of the Earth bulge out toward the sun as the Earth spins around. This causes night and day. And different parts of the Earth bulge out toward the sun as the Earth moves around the sun. This causes the seasons.

Let's take a closer look.

Let's take a closer look at the two ways the Earth moves. First, it spins around, like a top. It spins around on its *axis.* The Earth's axis is an imaginary line. It goes straight through the center of the Earth, and it comes out at the North Pole and South Pole.

You can make a model of the Earth and its axis. Just push a pencil through the middle of a ball of clay. The clay will be the Earth, and the pencil will be the Earth's axis. The top of the pencil will be the North Pole, and the bottom will be the South Pole.

11

As the Earth spins on its axis, the sun's rays light up the side of the Earth that is facing the sun. It is daytime on that side of the world. The other side of the Earth is in darkness. It is night on that side of the world. As the Earth spins, different parts of the world keep moving from darkness into light, and from light into darkness. That's why we have night and day.

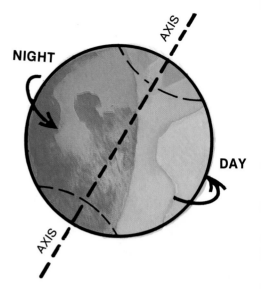

Now let's look at the second way the Earth moves. The Earth is constantly moving in a path around the sun. This path is called an *orbit.* It takes the Earth one year—365 days—to make one full journey around the sun. Then the trip begins again. As the Earth spins and travels around the sun, it does something else—it tilts, or leans, at a certain angle. As it travels, the part of the Earth tilting toward the sun has summer. The part tilting away from the sun has winter.

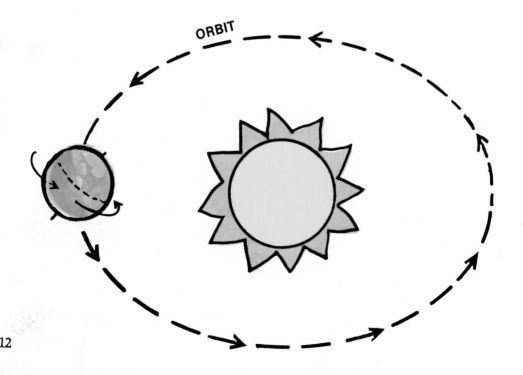

Try this experiment.

You can use your model of the Earth in an experiment to see just how the Earth tilts and travels around the sun. You will need only a pen, a darkened room, a flashlight, and a friend. Use the pen to mark a line all the way around your model, halfway between the North Pole and the South Pole. This line is like the Earth's *equator*.

The equator is an imaginary line that circles the Earth, like a belt. It divides the Earth into two halves, called *hemispheres*. The one with the North Pole is called the Northern Hemisphere. The one with the South Pole is called the Southern Hemisphere.

In a darkened room, hold your model of the Earth so the North Pole is tilted a little bit toward the door of the room. It should be tilted at this angle throughout the experiment. Have your friend stand between you and the door, and shine the flashlight on your model of the Earth. The flashlight will be the sun.

Is the North Pole of your model tilted slightly toward the sun? It should be. Because of this tilt, the direct rays fall *above* the equator. Direct rays are brighter and warmer than slanted rays. So it is summer above the equator—in the Northern Hemisphere. The only rays that reach below the equator are very slanted rays. So it is winter in the Southern Hemisphere.

Now start moving in a circle around the sun. Your helper must also turn to follow your path around the sun, so that the beam of light keeps shining on your model of the Earth. Stop moving when you are a quarter of the way around. The North Pole should still be tilted at the same angle. Because of the way the Earth's axis is tilted, the sun's direct rays should now fall right on the equator. Slightly slanted rays fall above and below the equator now. It is now autumn in the Northern Hemisphere, and spring in the Southern Hemisphere.

Now move another quarter of the way around the sun. The North Pole should still be tilted at the same angle. Is it tilted toward the sun, or away from the sun? It should be tilted away from the sun. Because of this tilt, the direct rays of the sun fall *below* the equator. It is summer in the Southern Hemisphere. Only very slanted rays fall above the equator, so it is winter in the Northern Hemisphere.

If you move another quarter of the way around the sun, the direct rays will fall on the equator again. Slightly slanted rays will fall above and below the equator. It will be spring in the Northern Hemisphere, and autumn in the Southern Hemisphere.

Now complete your circle around the sun, so you are standing where you began. The Earth has made one full orbit around the sun. You have seen how the tilt and orbit of the Earth cause the four seasons.

You probably noticed that when the North Pole was tilted *toward* the sun, the South Pole was tilted *away*. And when the North Pole was tilted *away* from the sun, the South Pole was tilted *toward* it.

For six months, the sun's rays cannot reach the pole that is tilted away from the sun. It is very, very cold and dark where the sun's rays cannot reach. And for six months, the sun's rays shine all the time on the pole that is tilted toward the sun. But these rays are very, very slanted. Even though they shine for twenty-four hours a day, they do not bring much heat. That's why the areas around the poles are so cold. They are called the *Frigid Zones*. Frigid means very cold.

In spring and autumn, the sun's direct rays fall right on the equator. In summer and winter, they fall just above or just below the equator. So the area near the equator is very hot all year long. This area is called the *Torrid Zone.* Torrid means very hot.

Where do most of the world's people live?

Between the Torrid Zone and the Frigid Zones lie the *Temperate Zones*. Temperate means not too hot and not too cold. There are two Temperate Zones—the North Temperate Zone and the South Temperate Zone. Most of the people, plants, and animals in the world live in the two Temperate Zones.

The North Temperate Zone and the South Temperate Zone have the same kinds of seasons. But they are reversed. When it is winter in the north, it is summer in the south. When it is spring in the north, it is autumn in the south.

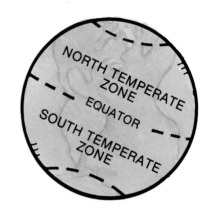

Do you live in the North Temperate Zone?

Many people do. Let's see what happens there during each season of the year. Suppose we start with the summer months—June, July, and August.

What are the signs of summer?

June 20 or 21 is the first day of summer in the North Temperate Zone. It is also the longest day of the year. The North Pole is tilted toward the sun. On this day, there will be far more hours of daylight than there are hours of darkness.

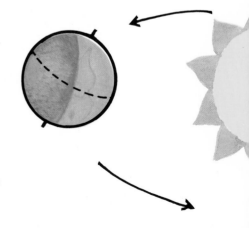

Summer is the time when plants grow best. Tomatoes get big and red and juicy in the sun. Corn ripens in the bright sunlight. Flowers bloom everywhere. It's good weather for swimming and camping and summer fun.

Bees buzz among the flowers. They are gathering nectar for honey. Butterflies dance from blossom to blossom. Crickets chirp noisily. The world is green and warm. The sun is high overhead, and it shines very brightly.

21

But there are also rainy days in the summer. The rain may spoil your fun, but plants need rain to grow. Sometimes there is a sudden thunderstorm. Thunder crashes, lightning flashes. Rain pours down, soaking into the warm soil. But these thunderstorms last just a short time. Afterward, the air feels a little cooler, and it smells very fresh.

First signs of autumn

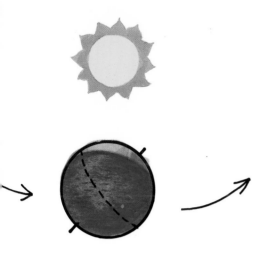

As the Earth moves around the sun, the days get shorter and cooler. The sun's rays hit the North Temperate Zone on more of a slant. Autumn is near. On September 22 or 23, the Earth has traveled a quarter of the way around the sun. The hours of sunlight and darkness are equal. This is called the *autumn equinox.* It is the first day of autumn.

September, October, and November are months for harvesting crops and getting ready for winter. By September, apples are ripe and ready to eat. Big orange pumpkins are made into Halloween jack-o'-lanterns. Wheat has been cut and stored, and the fields look bare and brown.

The trees are changing to their autumn colors. Their leaves are turning from green to red, yellow, orange, and gold. Soon they will be crisp and dry, and they will fall from the trees and crackle beneath your feet.

If you look at the sky, you may see flocks of birds flying south. Wild ducks and geese are the easiest to spot. They fly in long V-formations, on their way to warmer lands.

23

Around the middle of September, you may be lucky enough to see a wonderful sight. That is the time thousands of monarch butterflies gather for their long flight to California and Mexico, where they will spend the winter. They cling to low branches and bushes—and suddenly, they take to the air. They look like a beautiful, fluttering, orange-and-black cloud.

Squirrels and chipmunks scurry about, their cheeks bulging with nuts and acorns. They will hide these foods in hollow trees and in holes in the ground. They must store up enough food to last them all winter.

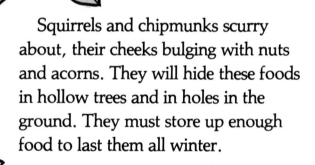

Bears eat their last big meals of the year. As soon as it grows really cold, they will settle down in a cave or hollow log, where they will sleep through much of the winter.

What are the signs of winter?

Now the Earth has traveled halfway around the sun. The northern end of the Earth's axis is tilted away from the sun, and only very slanted rays of sunshine reach us. The days are very cold. December 21 or 22 is the shortest day of the year. There will be far more hours of darkness than there are hours of daylight. After that, the sun will shine a little bit longer each day. But you will hardly notice, because the winter nights seem so long.

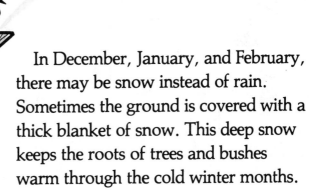

In December, January, and February, there may be snow instead of rain. Sometimes the ground is covered with a thick blanket of snow. This deep snow keeps the roots of trees and bushes warm through the cold winter months.

Most trees and bushes have lost all their leaves. But if you look closely at their branches, you will see tight little buds, waiting to open up in the spring. Many lakes and rivers have frozen over. But fish swim lazily at the bottom, where the water does not freeze.

Bears and woodchucks snooze through most of the winter. The extra food they ate in autumn has been stored as fat in their bodies. Now their bodies slowly use up this stored food.

On cold winter days, squirrels and chipmunks dig out the nuts and acorns they hid during autumn. Without these winter food supplies, they might not survive. Most insects have died, but they have left eggs or cocoons that will hatch into young insects in the spring.

26

Everywhere, the world seems to be waiting. You snuggle under your covers at night, and dream of warm sunny days. The winter has been fun, with skating and sledding and building people made of snow. And it has been beautiful, with drifting snow and sparkling icicles. But you are ready for a change. And a change is coming.

First signs of spring

By the middle of March, the bears have come out of their dens, looking for food. They are thin and hungry. They will even eat the moss on trees, if they can find nothing else. But soon they will see delicious green shoots of plants, poking through the ground. Spring has come.

In late March, it hardly feels like spring at all. It is
still cold. But there are fat buds on the branches of the
trees. The days have grown much longer than they were
in December. On March 20 or 21, there are again
twelve hours of daylight and twelve hours of darkness.
It is the *spring equinox*. The Earth has traveled three-
quarters of the way around the sun.

Grass is beginning to look greener. Trees are sprouting blossoms and tiny green leaves. The first spring flowers are starting to bloom.

Everything around you seems to be waking up. Animals are frisky—and you feel that way, too. You want to run and jump and shout. Winter is over, and spring is here at last!

Spring is a busy time. There are fields to be plowed and crops to be planted. Butterflies are fluttering back to their summer homes. Great flocks of birds have begun their return flights from their winter feeding grounds. Soon they will be building nests for their new families.

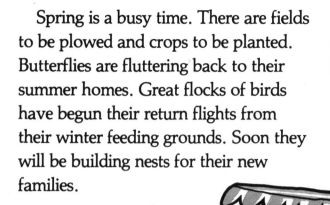

Spring is also a time of birth. The warm air is filled with the sounds of newborn calves, baby lambs, little piglets, and fuzzy ducklings. Insects are beginning to hatch. Hungry caterpillars crawl about, looking for food.

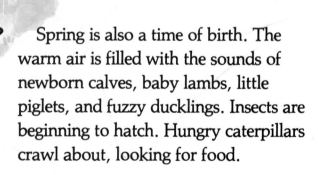

Every day gets a little longer and a little warmer. The leaves on the trees grow bigger every day. Flowers bloom everywhere.

The Earth has traveled all the way around the sun. Now the northern end of its axis is again tilted toward the sun. Summer has returned!

31

The sun keeps shining.

It sends out heat and light. The Earth keeps moving. It spins on its tilted axis as it travels around the sun.

And the seasons come and go with a beautiful rhythm. Summer. Autumn. Winter. Spring.